I0822612

The Father of Geometry

Euclid and His 3-D World

Titles in the *Great Minds of Ancient Science and Math* Series:

THE GREATEST MATHEMATICIAN:
ARCHIMEDES AND HIS EUREKA! MOMENT
ISBN-13: 978-0-7660-3408-2

THE GREATEST THINKER:
ARISTOTLE AND THE FOUNDATIONS OF SCIENCE
ISBN-13: 978-0-7660-3121-0

THE FATHER OF THE ATOM:
DEMOCRITUS AND THE NATURE OF MATTER
ISBN-13: 978-0-7660-3410-5

MEASURING THE EARTH:
ERATOSTHENES AND HIS CELESTIAL GEOMETRY
ISBN-13: 978-0-7660-3120-3

THE FATHER OF GEOMETRY:
EUCLID AND HIS 3-D WORLD
ISBN-13: 978-0-7660-3409-9

THE FATHER OF ANATOMY:
GALEN AND HIS DISSECTIONS
ISBN-13: 978-0-7660-3880-1

THE GREATEST DOCTOR OF ANCIENT TIMES:
HIPPOCRATES AND HIS OATH
ISBN-13: 978-0-7660-3118-0

THE GREAT PHILOSOPHER:
PLATO AND HIS PURSUIT OF KNOWLEDGE
ISBN-13: 978-0-7660-3119-7

THE FATHER OF GEOMETRY

EUCLID AND HIS 3-D WORLD

Paul Hightower

Enslow Publishers, Inc.
40 Industrial Road
Box 398
Berkeley Heights, NJ 07922
USA
http://www.enslow.com

Library of Congress Cataloging-in-Publication Data

Hightower, Paul (Paul W.)
    The father of geometry : Euclid and his 3-D world / Paul Hightower.
       p. cm. — (Great minds of ancient science and math)
    Summary: "A biography of ancient Greek mathematician Euclid, known as the father of geometry and author of the mathematics textbook Elements"—Provided by publisher.
    Includes bibliographical references and index.
    ISBN 978-0-7660-3409-9
    1. Euclid—Juvenile literature. 2. Mathematicians—Greece—Biography—Juvenile literature.
    3. Mathematics, Greek—Juvenile literature. 4. Geometry—History—Juvenile literature. I. Title.
    QA29.E78H54 2010
    510.92—dc22
    [B]
                                                2009023814

Printed in the United States of America

052010 Lake Book Manufacturing, Inc., Melrose Park, IL

10 9 8 7 6 5 4 3 2 1

To Our Readers: We have done our best to make sure all Internet addresses in this book were active and appropriate when we went to press. However, the author and the publisher have no control over and assume no liability for the material available on those Internet sites or on other Web sites they may link to. Any comments or suggestions can be sent by e-mail to comments@enslow.com or to the address on the back cover.

♻ Enslow Publishers, Inc., is committed to printing our books on recycled paper. The paper in every book contains 10% to 30% post-consumer waste (PCW). The cover board on the outside of each book contains 100% PCW. Our goal is to do our part to help young people and the environment too!

Illustration Credits: © AISA/The Everett Collection, Inc., pp. 21, 23; © Jupiterimages Corporation/Photos.com, p. 74; Enslow Publishers, Inc., pp. 10, 12, 32, 52, 70; The Granger Collection, New York, pp. 3, 9, 15, 58, 62, 64; Images courtesy History of Science Collections, University of Oklahoma Libraries, pp. 72, 86, 87; O.V.D./Shutterstock, p. 56; Sheila Terry/Photo Researchers, Inc., p. 48

Cover Illustration: The Granger Collection, New York.

CONTENTS

PRONUNCIATION GUIDE

Boethius—bow-EE-thee-us

Bolyai—BULL-yie

dodecahedron—doe-deck-uh-HEE-dren

Euclid—YOU-klid

Euclidean—you-KLID-ee-an

Hippocrates—he-POCK-rah-tees

icosahedron—eye-coe-suh-HEE-dren

Leibniz—LAIB-nitz

Lobachevsky—low-buh-CHEF-ski

octahedron—oct-uh-HEE-dren

Ptolemy—TOLL-uh-me

Pythagoras—pie-THAG-or-us

quadrivium—kwa-DRIV-ee-um

Riemann—REE-mahn

tetrahedron—tet-rah-HEE-dren

Thales—THAY-lees

Theaetetus—thee-ee-TEE-tus

THE LIFE OF EUCLID

EUCLID IS PROBABLY THE MOST FAMOUS person you may never have known. He was not a great general, leading an ancient army across the Roman Empire. He was not a great statesman or leader of one of the ancient Greek city-states. The names of Socrates and Plato and Archimedes are recognized by everyone, but Euclid is not as widely known.

At the end of his life, Euclid had not conquered his enemies. He did not build great temples or monuments to Greek gods or heroes. He did not invent great war machines to defend his fellow citizens under attack. He did not establish an academy or a philosophy or even write that many books. Yet Euclid achieved just as much or more than these other ancient men.

What Euclid did accomplish was writing a single, very important book. This book was not entirely original, as some of its ideas were borrowed from other writers. However, it was so well organized that it established a method of mathematics that has lasted for more than two thousand years. No other book except perhaps the Bible or the Koran has been so widely circulated, edited, and studied all over the world.[1]

Who Was Euclid?

Studying the life of Euclid is very difficult. Almost nothing is known about the details of his life. We have no definite dates for Euclid's birth or his death, nor do we know for certain where he was born or where he died. We do not know anything about his family or his children or even if he had a family at all. We do not know what he looked like or anything about his personality.

What we do know about Euclid are the books he wrote. Euclid wrote a book about mathematics and geometry called the *Elements*. The *Elements* formed the foundation of ancient Greek mathematics.[2] This book was so important and

This nineteenth-century engraving depicts what Euclid might have looked like. The Greek geometer lived about 300 B.C.

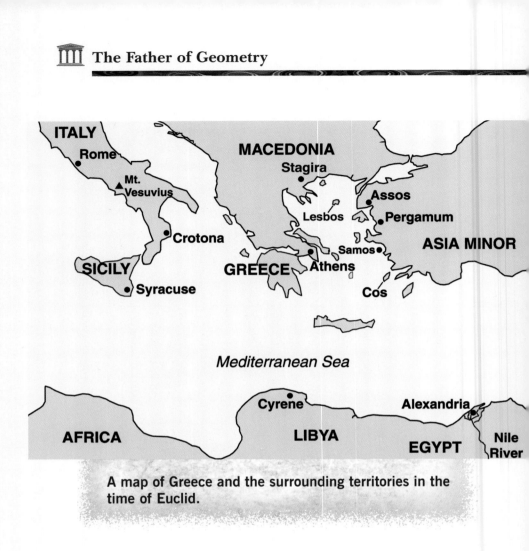

A map of Greece and the surrounding territories in the time of Euclid.

written so well, its organization made it fundamental to geometry. It was used as a student textbook almost unchanged for thousands of years.

Euclid was Greek, but he might have been born in Egypt.[3] Common dates given for his birth are about 320 B.C. and for his death about 270 B.C., but neither one of these is definite. Other ancient authors, such as Proclus, implied that Euclid taught in Alexandria, Egypt, for a time and that he wrote several other books. Thus, he is sometimes referred to as Euclid of Alexandria.

Euclid's World

To understand Euclid, we must understand the world in which he lived. He was preceded by the great Greek philosopher Plato (427–347 B.C.), and he lived after another Greek philosopher, Aristotle (384–322 B.C.). Plato founded the Academy in Athens and taught many other students and scholars. This was a golden age for Greek philosophy and learning, and the study of mathematics flourished.

It was the fourth century B.C., and the Greek city-states were rising as political powers. The Macedonian king Philip II (382–336 B.C.) brought many of these independent city-states under his control. Later his son Alexander

The Renaissance artist Raphael painted the Greek philosophers Plato (left) and Aristotle (right) in this 1509 work called *School of Athens.* Euclid lived after both of these great thinkers, whose writings influenced Western culture for centuries after their deaths.

(356–323 B.C.), known as "Alexander the Great," expanded Greek influence by conquering the Persian Empire—what is today called the Middle East. Alexander built a powerful empire that stretched all the way to India.

Conquering the Persian Empire, Alexander freed Egypt from Persian control. He was welcomed as a liberator by the Egyptians. Alexander founded the city of Alexandria at the mouth of the Nile River. Alexandria would become the biggest city in Egypt and a major trading post between Europe and Asia. It also served as the center for Greek influence in the Nile Valley.

After Alexander's sudden death in 323 B.C., his empire was divided among his officers. His general Ptolemy, also known as Ptolemy I or Ptolemy Soter, was one of Alexander's most trusted friends. Ptolemy claimed Egypt for his own and built a dynasty there that lasted for several centuries. Ptolemy's son and grandson were named Ptolemy II and Ptolemy III, and they also later ruled Egypt.

The Library of Alexandria

Some ancient authors claim Euclid was a childhood friend of Ptolemy's family, now the new rulers of Egypt.[4] The Ptolemys wanted to make Alexandria an important city of learning and research, so they established a great museum and a great library at Alexandria. The museum was to become a center of research and teaching after Alexander's empire fell apart.

Ptolemy invited Euclid to study and teach mathematics at the museum. The Alexandrian museum and library flourished under the Ptolemy family. Ptolemy required that all books brought to Alexandria by travelers or merchants be given to the library. At its peak, the library is estimated to have contained five hundred thousand scrolls.[5]

This library at Alexandria was more than just a collection of books. It was a center for lectures and teaching, similar to our modern universities. Alexandria was at a crossroads of commerce and travel. Many people from many countries passed through this city, and knowledge was learned from them and shared with them.

An artist's concept of a hall from the library in Alexandria. Many historians believe Euclid spent most of his life teaching at the library.

It is believed that Euclid may have spent most of his life in Alexandria. He taught mathematics to many students and wrote his books. We do not know how long he spent teaching at the library, but it may have been most of his life. We do not know if he ever traveled outside of Egypt, or if he stayed there until the day he died. Euclid taught at the library long enough for other ancient writers to know about his talent for mathematics.

Major Sources for Euclid

Only a few sources survive that tell us about Euclid's life. One is from Proclus (circa A.D. 411–485), a Greek philosopher who lived in Athens. Proclus wrote a book called the *Commentaries* that described Euclid as "younger than the pupils of Plato, but older than Eratosthenes and Archimedes."[6] Proclus did not have direct knowledge of Euclid or of his life or birthplace. However, he did note that Euclid "lived in the time of the first Ptolemy."

Another Greek mathematician who wrote about Euclid was Pappus of Alexandria (circa A.D. 290–350). Pappus organized and wrote about the works of other mathematicians, much as Euclid did. Many of the original works of Pappus survive, giving us some valuable sources for ancient Greek mathematics. Pappus wrote in his book *Collection* about students of Euclid's who lived in Alexandria.[7]

Our most direct sources for Euclid and his work are his own book, the *Elements*. The *Elements* was not actually published as a book as we know books today. Instead, it was a collection of thirteen individual scrolls, or parchments, each focused on a different topic of mathematics. Taken together, the *Elements* are considered as one book divided into thirteen chapters.

None of the original manuscripts of Euclid's *Elements* survives today. We only know about these ancient works because they were copied almost immediately. These copies were used as textbooks to teach other students about mathematics. Copies of the *Elements* were translated into different languages and carried to other countries. Because so many copies were made, the contents of the original book are preserved for us to read today.

As we know so little about the man named Euclid, our best understanding of him is through his work. By studying his books of the *Elements* and their concepts, we can discover a little about how Euclid thought. We may never know if Euclid had any descendants but we do know his legacy of the *Elements* and its value to mathematics.

Geometry
Before Euclid

THE ORIGINS OF GEOMETRY DID NOT come from pure mathematics. Before Euclid, geometry was used by the Egyptians to figure out their taxes. Because the Nile River flooded every year, landowners paid taxes to the pharaoh based on the area they owned. Simple geometry was used to calculate the shape of their land.[1] The word *geometry* comes from the Greek words *geo* meaning "earth" and *metron* meaning "measure."

Geometry is a part of mathematics that deals with shapes, lines, points, and angles. These objects can have very specific and detailed relationships between themselves and each other. These relationships are abstract, meaning they are not tied to one physical object like a desk or a chair. A relationship for a triangle or a square holds for all triangles or squares, no matter their size or location.

Today there are many branches of mathematics. Geometry is one of the oldest forms of mathematics because it does not depend on numbers. In ancient times, different civilizations used different symbols for numbers and values. The Greeks used a different numbering system than we use today. However, the basis for geometry is logical argument, not numbers. Geometry is the same in all languages because it uses only shapes, lines, and angles.

Greek Geometry

Euclid did not invent geometry. Other Greek mathematicians worked on various problems centuries before Euclid. Hippocrates of Chios (born about 470 B.C.) was the first Greek mathematician to write a book on geometry.[2] He wrote the book *Elements of Geometry* more than a century before Euclid was born. However, this book was lost and no copy has ever been found.

Mathematics before Euclid was centered around two other famous mathematicians. These

Thales of Miletus (above) is known as the first Greek philosopher, mathematician, and scientist. One of his many contributions to geometry is the method of deduction used to prove geometrical theorems.

21

two men were Thales of Miletus (c. 624–548 B.C.) and Pythagoras of Samos (c. 580–500 B.C.). We know even less about the lives of Thales and Pythagoras than we do about Euclid. Some ancient authors claim both these men traveled widely throughout the ancient world. All we really know about them is that they wrote about the mathematics they had learned.

Thales is regarded as the first Greek philosopher and the first true mathematician.[3] He settled in Ionia, a region that is today on the southwestern coast of modern-day Turkey, or Asia Minor. Thales is credited with bringing a deductive organization to geometry. Deduction is a logical step-by-step reasoning using basic concepts to prove more complex ideas. This method of deduction is central to all geometry theorems.

The School of Pythagoras

Pythagoras settled in a Greek part of Italy known then as Magna Graecia. He established the Pythagorean school, which was more of a

Pythagoras (above) and his followers believed that everything in the world could be understood using mathematics. Mathematics was more than just a discipline to the Pythagoreans; it was a way of life.

communal brotherhood than a teaching academy. The Pythagoreans lived together and shared everything, including mathematical discoveries. Credit for the mathematical writings of Pythagoras was never given to an individual but was shared with everyone in his school.

The Pythagoreans believed that "all is number," and that everything in the world, including philosophy, could be reduced to mathematics.[4] The Pythagoreans held an almost religious respect for the principles of mathematics. They regarded some numbers as holy, and they built their philosophy and way of life on these numbers.

The fifth century B.C. was the true birth of Greek mathematics. This was the age of the famous Greek philosophers, such as Socrates (c. 470–399 B.C.) and his student Plato. This is known as the "Golden Age," a time of relative success for Athens and other Greek city-states. Arts, literature, and the sciences thrived. During this time, many Greek mathematicians began to write books and form schools.

Euclid's Organization

The fame of Euclid did not come from his original writings. Most of the material from Euclid's first two chapters of the *Elements* might also be credited to the Pythagoreans.[5] Instead, Euclid took the ideas of geometry known at that time and organized them into a single, unified work. He applied a strict, logical attention to each proof. By providing a deductive proof for each mathematical concept, these ideas became very accurate and reliable.

Euclid introduced a logical, organized way of thinking about geometry. He built relationships about concepts based on basic principles called axioms. An axiom (also called postulate) is a statement that is commonly believed to be true without needing proof. Examples of axioms would be "Fish live in water," or "Triangles have three sides." There is no need to prove these statements, as they are considered true by themselves.

Using these axioms, Euclid built mathematical proofs called theorems. A theorem is a statement that has been logically proved to be true. Step-by-step, basic postulates and relationships would be linked together to prove the theorem. The difference between an axiom and a theorem is that the axiom is assumed to be true, but the theorem is proved to be true. Many theorems can be combined and used to prove more complex theorems.

Some modern scholars believe that Euclid took much of the *Elements* from principles of construction.[6] When building a house, you lay down the foundation, then construct the walls, then finish with the roof. The roof depends on the walls being strong, and the walls depend on a solid foundation. Similarly, a mathematical proof is built on each previous statement. If any previous step in a proof is not true, it will fall apart just like a house with a weak wall.

The *Elements*

Euclid's books of the *Elements* are more like chapters in a single text. Each part is called a "book" because it was a separate scroll or parchment, not a different book. These parts are organized and usually considered as a whole, as a single "book" written by Euclid. There are thirteen total parts, referred to by Roman numerals as Book I through Book XIII.

Book I through Book VI focus on the subject of plane geometry. This is the geometry with which you are most familiar, dealing with shapes, circles, lines, and angles. The basic postulates of geometry are established, and basic theorems are proved. These books serve as a guide for later proofs, when the subjects get more complex.

Book VII through Book IX deal with the subject of number theory. Number theory is different than geometry because it deals with integers and counting numbers. Euclid treated these numbers as geometric figures, and used his geometry proofs for these properties of numbers. Different subjects included here are infinite series of numbers, proportions, and prime numbers.

Book X is unique among the other chapters of Euclid's work. It is by far the longest chapter of the Elements, and its contents can be difficult to understand. This book focuses on a special class of numbers called irrational numbers, also known as "incommensurable" numbers. This is a complicated subject, and we will examine irrational numbers in a later chapter.

Like the first four books, Book XI through Book XIII again focus on geometry. But this topic is the geometry of solid objects, things like spheres, cubes, cylinders, and pyramids. These are objects in three dimensions, whereas plane geometry has just two dimensions. Three-dimensional shapes have properties and relationships of their own, just as two-dimensional shapes do.

Proclus described the *Elements* as having the same relation to mathematics as the letters of the alphabet have to language.[7] Euclid was able to detail a method of constructing proofs that could be used in other areas of mathematics, not just geometry. Other mathematical subjects use this same method of reasoning for their proofs.

Even today, Euclid's *Elements* remains the most successful textbook in the history of mathematics. It was written so well, later editions did not change much. The *Elements* was translated and copied for centuries. It was used as a teaching tool even until the nineteenth century, and today's schoolbooks are based on the same principles.

PLANE GEOMETRY

LOOK AT YOUR DINING-ROOM TABLE OR the surface of your desk. It is a level, smooth, flat surface, just like a piece of paper. Imagine the edges of this table getting longer, stretching out to fill the entire room. Now imagine the table going on forever, with edges that are infinitely long. This table has become a mathematical plane, an environment that includes only two dimensions.

In mathematics, a dimension is more like a direction, like north and south, or left and right. A plane is defined by only two dimensions, generally referred to as length and width. A flat piece of paper has length and width, so its surface is described as two-dimensional. Likewise, any shapes or designs that you can draw on this paper are also two-dimensional. They are included in the plane of the paper.

The first four chapters of Euclid's *Elements* focus on plane geometry, or the geometry in one flat plane. Each chapter deals with a different subject, and later chapters build on earlier work. When a theorem, or principle, is proved, it can be used to prove other theorems. In this way, more complicated ideas can be solidly built on top of simple ones.

What Is Plane Geometry?

Plane geometry is the study of shapes and principles within a two-dimensional plane. This also includes the geometric shapes that are included in such a plane, such as triangles, rectangles, and other shapes. Closed shapes that have a number of straight sides are described as polygons, meaning "many sides." Triangles, rectangles, and pentagons are all special names for these particular polygons.

Plane geometry includes the shapes known as conics. Conics are shapes produced when a flat,

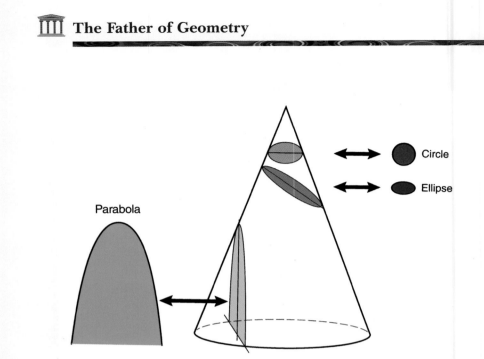

Parabola

Circle

Ellipse

This diagram shows the different shapes that result from cutting a cone at different angles. Conics include circles, ellipses, and parabolas.

two-dimensional plane intersects a three-dimensional cone. The shapes produced are included in that flat plane, such as circles, ellipses, and other curves. The study of conics is a detailed subsection of plane geometry.

Also included in plane geometry are angles and the relationships between lines. When two lines, or segments, intersect, they form an angle.

Different angles have different properties and relationships with the lines that form them. One special and important angle is called a right angle. An angle is a right angle if it is exactly equal to 90 degrees, or where two lines are perpendicular. The corners of a square are right angles.

Just as we have laws that govern our country and our city, mathematics also has laws. These laws define the relationships between different shapes, lines, and angles. Euclid did not invent these laws but he did collect and organize them. The work included in Book I and Book II is believed by some scholars to be originally from the Pythagoreans.[1]

Book I of the *Elements* begins with twenty-three basic definitions. Euclid defines simple things like a point, a line, a segment, or what is meant by "straight." These definitions may seem too obvious—of course, we all know what a line is! However, mathematics requires these explicit definitions so they can be used as building blocks for other concepts.

Following the definitions are Euclid's five postulates. These fundamental postulates form the foundation for all the geometry that will follow. The first four are:

1. A line segment can be drawn from any point to any other point.
2. A line segment can be extended indefinitely in either direction.
3. Given any point, a circle with a radius can be drawn with that point at its center.
4. All right angles are equal to each other.[2]

The fifth postulate is more complicated, and it has its own problems. We will explore this famous Fifth Postulate later.

After these postulates, Euclid offers five axioms, sometimes called "common notions." They are offered without proof, and they are assumed to be true. Euclid felt that these ideas were so basic, they were obvious to everyone. They are:

1. Two objects both equal to a third object are also equal to each other.

2. If equals are added to equals, the wholes are equal.

3. If equals are subtracted from equals, the remainders are equal.

4. Objects that coincide with one another are equal to one another.

5. The whole is greater than the part.[3]

These common notions are not so much geometry but logical principles that may be important later.

Book I continues with its introduction of the basic ideas of geometry with forty-eight postulates, or theorems. These detail the rules by which angles and areas can be proven equal. They explore the relationship between lines that are parallel to each other. They also prove properties of the angles included within a triangle, as well as other basic properties.

The Beginnings of Algebra

Book II is a short book, and is a continuation of the basic concepts of Book I. It has only fourteen propositions, and is sometimes called the book of "geometrical algebra."[4] Algebra is the branch of mathematics that deals with numbers, their relationships, and solving equations. The word *algebra* comes from a later Arabic term meaning "completion" or "restoration."[5] It is often used to solve equations for an unknown value.

The mathematics of algebra would not be developed for many centuries after Euclid. It is a subject that is filled with symbols that represent different operations and relationships. However, ancient Greek mathematics did not yet have these efficient mathematical symbols. Euclid wrote some of these same relationships using geometry.

For example, we today write "$1+1=2$," where the numbers "1" and "2" have some values and the other symbols "$+$" and "$=$" indicate operations or relationships. However, the Greeks would write, "One line segment added to another segment of the same length is equal to a final segment of twice the original length." The meaning is the same but the idea is presented with geometric ideas rather than numbers.

Circles and Angles

Through the first two books, the *Elements* only deals with points, lines, segments, and angles. These objects can be combined to form more complex shapes. Polygons are just figures made up of line segments and angles. A triangle has three segments and three angles, with *tri* meaning "three." A pentagon has five segments and five angles, with *penta* meaning "five."

Book III begins the discussion of circles and their properties, and includes thirty-seven propositions. It also begins with eleven definitions, such as a tangent to a circle. A tangent is a straight line that touches a circle in just one point, never passing through it. Other relationships between circles and angles, and circles and other circles are proven here.

Book IV is another short book, containing only sixteen propositions. It continues the discussion about circles but has more problems worked out than it has basic principles. This book deals with inscribing or circumscribing circles around other polygons. Inscribing means the circle is drawn inside the figure, and circumscribing means the circle is drawn outside the figure.

The contents of Book III and Book IV are assumed to be originally from Hippocrates of Chios.[6] Hippocrates also wrote a book called *Elements of Geometry,* but this was not the same as Euclid's book. Euclid may have used the same ideas as Hippocrates but wrote them as formal theorems. What Euclid introduced was not the mathematical concepts themselves but a method for writing and proving them.

THE THEORY OF NUMBERS

ALTHOUGH EUCLID FOCUSED MAINLY ON topics of geometry, he also wrote about other mathematics. Right in the middle of the *Elements,* he devotes several chapters to non-geometry subjects. Like the rest of the chapters, these topics were largely taken from other sources and organized by Euclid. No one knows why he wrote the *Elements* this way.

At this time, Greek mathematics was very basic. They did not have algebra nor did they have trigonometry, and they only barely knew geometry. Mathematics was just beginning to branch off from logic and philosophy as its own separate subject. It was growing from a practical tool used for building ships and calculating taxes to an abstract area of pure mathematics.

The Pythagoreans and later Plato believed in what was called the quadrivium, which is Latin for "the four roads." The quadrivium was a course of study believed essential for educated people. It consisted of four subjects: geometry, arithmetic, astronomy, and music.[1] Euclid wrote books on all these subjects, with geometry and arithmetic as the focus of the *Elements*.

What Is Number Theory?

Number theory (sometimes also called arithmetic) is the field of mathematics that deals with numbers and their relationships. This may sound strange, as we all know what numbers are—we use them every day. But numbers have relationships with each other the same way geometric shapes do. These relationships must be stated and proven using theorems similar to those in geometry.

Book V of the *Elements* includes eighteen new definitions and twenty-five propositions. It focuses on the theory of magnitudes and ratios, where a ratio is a measure of the relative size of two values. Ratios are written as fractions of whole numbers, such as $^3/_4$ or $^9/_{25}$. Ratios are important because they can describe a relationship between the size of two similar items. Two similar triangles may be different sizes, and their relative sizes can be expressed exactly as a ratio of two whole numbers.

Ratios become even more important when combined as proportions. A proportion is setting two ratios equal to each other. Using proportions, unknown values can be solved in incomplete ratios. Euclid organized and presented these basic postulates, even though he did not invent them. The mathematician Eudoxus of Cnidus (born about 408 B.C.) discovered almost the whole contents of Book V of the *Elements* long before Euclid.[2]

Proportions and Numbers

Book V and Book VI apply the theory of proportions to geometry. Book VI includes thirty-three propositions in which Euclid represented numbers as lengths, or magnitudes. Treating these magnitudes as geometric figures, he deduced their properties from the laws of geometry.[3] In this way, Euclid was able to treat number theory using methods similar to geometry, with which he was much more familiar.

Book VII has twenty-two new definitions about numbers and thirty-nine propositions. This book is an introduction to elementary number theory, proving some basic principles about numbers. Some scholars believe that the topics of Book VII through Book IX of the *Elements* were originally taken from a Pythagorean text.[4]

For example, this book deals with two concepts of proportion called the greatest common divisor and the least common multiple. The greatest common divisor (GCD) is the largest factor that is common between two whole numbers. For example, the number 12 has divisors 1, 2, 3, 4 and 6, and the number 20 has divisors 1, 2, 4, 5 and 10. The largest divisor these two numbers have in common is 4, so the GCD of 12 and 20 is 4.

Determining the GCD for small numbers is rather simple. We can list out the factors and compare them directly. But for large numbers, this method becomes too complicated. Euclid worked out a shortcut called Euclid's method for finding the GCD. Using this approach, a GCD between any two numbers can be found quickly, without listing out all factors.

The least common multiple (LCM) is the smallest whole number of which both of two numbers are a divisor. Using our previous example, the multiples of 12 are 24, 36, 48, 60, 72, 84 and so on. The multiples of 20 are 40, 60, 80, 100 and so on. The LCM is the smallest number these two values have in common, which is 60 in this case. Euclid also included a method for finding the LCM in Book VII.

Prime Numbers

Also included in Book VII are some properties of prime numbers. A prime number is a number that only has divisors of itself and 1. Examples of prime numbers are 5, 19, 23 and 137. The number 23 has no factors other than 1 and 23. Prime numbers are unique and have been studied as a curiosity by mathematicians for centuries. Euclid also demonstrated that the number of prime numbers is infinite.[5]

Book VIII has twenty-seven propositions and studies series of numbers that increase proportionally. Some number series have the property that each value increases by a certain proportion as they progress. Such series are known as geometric series, and their values quickly get very large. This series could continue forever, becoming an infinite series. Euclid explores the properties of geometric series of numbers in this book.

Book IX continues the applications of Book VII and Book VIII with thirty-six more propositions. Included in Book IX are topics such as adding together geometric series, and the concept of perfect numbers. Perfect numbers are whole numbers whose value is equal to the sum of their divisors. For example, the factors of 28 are 1, 2, 4, 7 and 14, and $1+2+4+7+14=28$, making 28 a "perfect" number.

The ancient Pythagoreans believed these perfect numbers had special mystical properties. During their time, they only discovered the first four perfect numbers: 6, 28, 496 and 8128. Today, mathematicians use computers to study many more perfect numbers after these first four values that become extremely large.

"Incommensurables"

Book X has been called the most "perfect" of all the books in the *Elements*.[6] It deals with what the Greeks called "incommensurable" magnitudes, or what are today called irrational numbers. Rational numbers can be expressed as a ratio of two whole numbers. The values $1/4$, $5/16$ or $156/240$ are all rational numbers, and all have definite equivalent decimal values (0.25, 0.3125 and 0.65, respectively).

On the other hand, irrational numbers cannot be written as a ratio of two whole numbers. Their equivalent decimal values continue infinitely and without repeating. The numbers $\pi = 3.14159...$, $e = 2.71828...$ and $\sqrt{2} = 1.4142...$ are all examples of irrational numbers.

Because the decimal digits continue forever, the values of these numbers can only be written as approximates. Instead, symbols such as π and e are used to represent these numbers.

Book X includes sixteen definitions and 115 propositions, more than any of the other chapters in the *Elements*.[7] Many of these topics may appear useless at first glance. Some are little more than mathematical oddities, studied for their own curious properties. However, a few have practical applications in science and engineering. Any method that can prove or shorten an otherwise complex mathematical problem is a good tool to have.

Solid Geometry

MANY SCHOLARS BELIEVE EUCLID WAS A friend of Ptolemy, the ruler of Egypt. He may have even been a teacher to the Ptolemy family. A story is told by Proclus that Ptolemy once asked Euclid for a shorter or easier way to learn geometry instead of studying the *Elements*. Euclid replied, "There is no royal road to geometry," meaning that studying mathematics has no easy path.[1]

The many topics of the *Elements* can sometimes be difficult. The concepts get ever more complicated the further you read into this series of books. However, there are no shortcuts for this area of mathematics. The geometry you learn at school is the same geometry that kings, generals, and presidents must learn when they study at school.

This illustration from the nineteenth-century French book *Vies des Savants Illustres* ("Lives of Famous Scientists") shows Euclid, wearing a red cloak, presenting a copy of *Elements* to Ptolemy, seated on the throne. There were no shortcuts to learning geometry, not even for a king. Anyone who wanted to learn geometry had to study the *Elements*.

One topic that becomes more complex is when the mathematics is expanded to three dimensions. Triangles and squares exist within a two-dimensional piece of paper. But we live in a three-dimensional world, one with length, width, and height. Shapes in our three-dimensional world are called solids, and they have a special geometry all their own.

What Is Solid Geometry?

Recall that plane geometry deals with shapes and figures in a two-dimensional plane. Solid geometry deals with solid shapes, or objects in three-dimensional space. A photograph of an apple exists in two dimensions, having only length and width on a piece of paper. A real apple is a solid, three-dimensional shape with length, width, and height.

Solid geometry is a continuation of plane geometry, as every two-dimensional shape is similar to a solid object. A circle in three dimensions in called a sphere, and a square in three dimensions is called a cube. But the world of solids has even more objects, and some can be very complicated. Some three-dimensional solids are made up of combinations of two-dimensional shapes.

Book XI returns to a discussion of geometry, with twenty-eight new definitions and thirty-nine propositions. It generalizes Book I through Book VI to three-dimensional space, with each shape having a solid counterpart. Each of these solids has properties and relationships just as two-dimensional shapes do. Each of these solids also has additional properties that two-dimensional shapes do not, such as volume and surface area.

The Method of Exhaustion

Book XII of the *Elements* contains eighteen propositions, and details an important method for calculating the area of a circle. Calculating the area of a regular polygon is rather simple. All the straight sides and similar angles mean the shape's area can be worked out as the sum of smaller shapes. Any larger shape can be broken into smaller pieces, and finding the area of these smaller pieces is simple. However, measuring the area of a circle is a little more difficult.

If you inscribe a polygon within a circle, the area of the polygon can be used as an approximation of the area of the circle. The difference is only the gap left between the sides of the polygon and the circle. As the number of sides of this inscribed polygon increases, the gap left between the polygon and the circle decreases. The approximate area calculated by the polygon becomes closer to the true area of the circle.

This method probably came from the earlier mathematician Eudoxus.[2] It is called the method of exhaustion because the inscribed polygon with an increasing number of sides is used to "exhaust" the area of the circle. This is a very powerful concept, and Euclid including it in the *Elements* influenced others to continue developing this method.

Other mathematicians such as Archimedes would also write and improve this method of exhaustion. As the number of sides of the

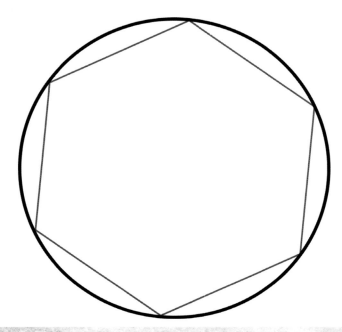

The method of exhaustion is used to approximate the area of a circle. First, you draw a polygon inside a circle. Then, you calculate the area of the polygon. The greater the number of sides of the polygon, the closer the polygon's area would be to the area of the circle.

inscribed polygon approaches infinity, the area of the polygon should exactly equal the area of the circle. This method formed the basis of the mathematics today known as calculus. However, calculus would be developed by the English mathematician Sir Isaac Newton (1642–1727) and the German mathematician Gottfried Wilhelm Leibniz (1646–1716) almost two thousand years later.

Philosophy and Perfection

The last book, Book XIII, is entirely devoted to studying a few special solids. These regular solids are unique shapes, and only five of them exist. Much of the work for this last book probably comes from the earlier Greek mathematician Theaetetus (c. 417–369 B.C.).[3] His work was known to the great teacher and philosopher Plato, who named one of his books *Theaetetus* in honor of the mathematician.

Plato is today known more as a philosopher, not a mathematician. However, he lived and died before Euclid, or at most around the same time as the mathematician. Plato regarded learning mathematics just as important as learning philosophy. The logical thinking of geometry is important to philosophical thinking. Plato inscribed the words, "Let no one ignorant of geometry enter here," over the entry doors of his academy.[4]

Because he was focused on philosophy rather than geometry, Plato tried to make sense of his world. At that time, the four basic elements of nature were considered very important. These elements were earth, air, fire, and water. Plato thought that perfect geometric shapes could be associated with each of these elements.

A "perfect geometric shape" is a three-dimensional object with sides made up only of identical two-dimensional shapes. For example, a cube has sides that are all perfect squares. No other shapes are used to construct a cube, and all the sides are equal. Plato believed that this mathematical solid was "perfect" and worthy of further study.

The Five Platonic Solids

Only five such perfect solids are known. These are the only objects than can be constructed from similar shapes. Each is named after the number of sides it contains:

- The tetrahedron, or a four-sided pyramid made up of equilateral triangles
- The cube, a six-sided box made up of squares
- The octahedron, an eight-sided object made up of equilateral triangles
- The dodecahedron, a twelve-sided object made up of regular pentagons
- The icosahedron, a twenty-sided object also made up of equilateral triangles.

Some of these objects were probably discovered earlier by the Pythagoreans. Plato wrote about these five solids in his book *Timaeus*. Because Plato wrote about them, they are often called the five Platonic solids.[5] These Platonic solids are unique and have been studied by both philosophers and mathematicians for centuries.

Euclid examined the properties of these Platonic solids in the eighteen propositions in Book XIII of the *Elements*. The final proposition in this last book was used to prove that these five were the only perfect solids, and that no more existed to be discovered.[6] Some examples of

This graphic shows four out of the five Platonic solids: (left to right) tetrahedron, icosahedron, dodecahedron, octahedron. The fifth solid, not shown here, is the cube.

these perfect solids are found in nature, especially in the microscopic structure of crystals. Because of their own symmetry, these Platonic solids were regarded as having almost mystical properties.

Altogether, Euclid used his twenty-three definitions, five postulates, and five common notions to prove a total of 465 theorems in the *Elements*.[7] At the time, this was all the knowledge of geometry known to the ancient world. Euclid wrote it all so clearly that with very few changes it was used by students everywhere studying geometry.

EUCLID'S PARALLEL POSTULATE

IN THE EARLY NINETEENTH CENTURY, two European mathematicians made similar discoveries at about the same time. János Bolyai (1802–1860), a Hungarian mathematician, developed the same idea that the Russian mathematician Nikolai Ivanovich Lobachevsky (1792–1856) did. Both men worked out a system of mathematics that proved Euclid wrong.

At that time, speaking against Euclid was almost like speaking against mathematics itself. Euclid's work had been accepted as true for almost two thousand years. Other mathematicians could not accept the idea that Euclid made mistakes, especially large ones like these. If Euclid was proven incorrect, the truth of the whole field of mathematics would be questioned.

The Russian mathematician Nikolai Ivanovich Lobachevsky was one of the founders of non-Euclidean geometry.

Both Bolyai and Lobachevsky published their work. But Lobachevsky was published in a small journal that few mathematicians ever read. Bolyai's work was buried in the appendix of a larger book on mathematics.[1] No one took any notice, and their work was eventually overlooked. It was not until a more famous mathematician proved them correct that their ideas were noticed at all.

The Fifth Postulate

Euclid's Fifth Postulate is introduced in the first book of the *Elements,* and has proven to be the most controversial. It was an original concept written by Euclid, not one copied from a previous author.[2] This postulate was not used very often in proofs, and mathematicians for centuries were uncomfortable with its ideas.

The Fifth Postulate states: "Given a line segment that crosses two lines in a way that the sum of their inner angles on the same side is less than two right angles, then the lines will eventually meet."[3] Basically, this is a test to measure whether two lines are parallel. Parallel means that two lines are spaced perfectly apart at all points, and that they never intersect.

If the segment that crosses the lines forms right angles, the lines must be parallel. If the sum of the inner angles are not equal to the sum of two right angles, no matter how small the difference, the two lines will eventually converge at some point. This postulate provides a definition for parallel lines, thus it is also called the Parallel Postulate.

Unproven or Flawed?

Euclid left this postulate unproven. He must have felt that this result was clearly true like other axioms, and needed no detailed proof. Or Euclid might have been unable to prove it, relying instead on its rather obvious nature. Many mathematicians since Euclid believed that this postulate needed proof and should have been written as a theorem. They thought it was not very obvious.

Many famous mathematicians tried to prove Euclid's Fifth Postulate. A Greek mathematician named Claudius Ptolemaeus (also called Ptolemy but no relation to the Egyptian rulers) made the first attempt at a proof but his proof was mistaken. Proclus, another Greek mathematician, offered a proof only a few centuries after Euclid, but his proof was also flawed. The Arab scholar Thābit ibn Qurrah (A.D. 826–901) also tried a proof in the ninth century A.D., but he also failed.

In the year 1663, an English mathematician named John Wallis (1616–1703) introduced yet another proof of the Parallel Postulate. Wallis's proof involved using properties of similar triangles, or triangles of different sizes but with the same interior angles. His proof was never accepted by other mathematicians because they did not see it as a working solution.[4] However, the one element that Wallis did introduce publicly was the idea that Euclid's postulate might be wrong.

For Euclid to be wrong was an almost impossible thought. Euclid's work had been studied and used for mathematical proofs for

The English mathematician John Wallis constructed a proof that demonstrated how Euclid's postulate could be incorrect.

almost two thousand years. It was not until the great German mathematician Carl Friedrich Gauss (1777–1855) tried to prove Euclid's Fifth Postulate that the next great discovery in geometry was made.

Gauss's New Math

What Gauss had developed was a series of relationships for triangles that was true but contradicted Euclid's theorems. In this case, Euclid was correct but so was Gauss, even though they proved opposite properties about triangles. Which mathematician had the true proof, the ancient Greek or the modern genius? The answer was that both of them did.

Gauss discovered that Euclid's proofs worked for a certain type of space. This space was named Euclidean space, and it has the common dimensions of length, width, and height. All these dimensions are at right angles, like the inside corner of a box. All Euclid's theorems and mathematics work for all shapes, lines, and angles included in Euclidean space.

The German mathematician Carl Friedrich Gauss discovered that Euclid's theorems worked in a specific type of space called Euclidean space, but they did not hold true in non-Euclidean space. Euclid was not completely wrong, nor was he completely right.

However, there is also a type of space called non-Euclidean space. This space has similar dimensions but not at right angles. It is curved in different directions, like the surface of a sphere. Think of a triangle drawn on a balloon with a pen. As you inflate the balloon, the dimensions and the angles of the triangle change. They become curved, and Euclid's theorems are no longer true. The skin of the balloon is a non-Euclidean surface.

It was not until the nineteenth century that mathematicians accepted the "flawed" status of Euclid's Fifth Postulate. Gauss never published his work, but he did write letters to Bolyai and Lobachevsky. After Gauss died, his work became known and other mathematicians had to accept this different idea of space. Gauss's work was the basis for the formulation of non-Euclidean geometry.

Our Non-Euclidean Universe

Non-Euclidean geometry is closer to the real world than Euclid's original mathematics. Euclid's theorems work best for shapes within a perfectly flat plane. Some theorems also work for regular three-dimensional objects. But we do not live in a perfectly flat plane. For example, Earth is shaped like a large sphere, not a flat surface. Even though it looks flat, it is very slightly curved.

About the same time as Gauss, another mathematician began questioning Euclid's original work. A German mathematician by the name of Georg Friedrich Bernhard Riemann (1826–1866) began to reinterpret the basic definitions of geometry.[5] He formulated his own postulates about spheres and curved surfaces. Riemann built a theoretical, mathematical structure that was entirely non-Euclidean.

Later, Riemann's mathematics allowed another scientist to make a very important discovery. The German physicist Albert Einstein (1879–1955) used Riemann's non-Euclidean geometry to develop his own theories. He wrote that if you do not move in a straight line, "the laws that govern rigid bodies do not correspond to the rules of Euclidean geometry."[6] Einstein's theory of general relativity showed that space itself is curved, and non-Euclidean in nature. We live in a non-Euclidean universe.

However, just because our real world is non-Euclidean does not mean we should ignore Euclid's work. Both Euclidean geometry and non-Euclidean geometry are equally correct. Euclidean geometry is still true for certain situations, such as objects within a plane. The geometry, shapes, and angles you study on paper still follow the rules set forth by Euclid. And the methods of postulates, theorems, and logical deduction still hold.

7

EUCLID AND THE SCIENCES

AN OLD STORY IS RETOLD BY AN ANCIENT Greek writer named Stobaeus, who lived in the fifth century A.D. He writes of one of Euclid's geometry students asking his teacher a question. The student asks, "What advantage shall I get by learning these things?" Euclid tells his slave, "Give him threepence, since he must needs make profit out of what he learns."[1]

Euclid was trying to tell his student that knowledge is important for its own sake. Some knowledge you need to live your life—like how to drive a car or how to cook dinner or how to fix a house. Other knowledge is good to know to get a job, like how to fly an airplane or prescribe medicine. Many people spend years studying for certain advanced careers. But some knowledge is good to know just for itself. Everything we learn does not need to be tied to a profession or a reward.

Much of what Euclid wrote is not practical in our everyday world. However, he did write a few books on scientific topics. Euclid studied how we see things, and about how the eye interacts with light. He also wrote a little about astronomy, developing spherical geometry to model our solar system. Some historians believe Euclid also wrote about the mathematics behind music, although this original text is lost.[2]

Optics and Vision

Euclid had an interest in optics, which is the study of light and vision. He wrote about this subject in a book entitled *Optics*. Euclid examined human vision from a geometric perspective. He believed that rays of light follow straight lines to and from the human eye. These straight lines and the angles they make follow the laws of geometry, and can be studied mathematically.

This scene from Raphael's *School of Athens* depicts Euclid (low center, bent over, pointing to the ground) teaching a group of students. Euclid believed knowledge enriched people's lives, whether or not they applied what they learned to specific tasks.

This book by Euclid presented one of the first attempts to study optics mathematically. Euclid established important ideas of linear perspective, or how an object is viewed as different sizes and shapes at various distances. When you see people far away, they appear small. But when they are close, they appear much larger.

Euclid was more interested in this geometric basis than the nature of light itself. He studied the geometry and the angles of the rays of light. But Euclid did not examine the function of the human eye. He was not concerned with how light interacts with this organ, or how it is perceived by our minds.[3] Thus, this work was advanced in some ways and limited in others.

Euclid and the Stars

With his solid geometry, Euclid developed a system of coordinates around a sphere. A sphere requires a special case of coordinates to locate a point on its surface. This subject is called spherical geometry, or the study of the two-dimensional surface of a sphere. Euclid wrote an entire book about spherical geometry entitled *Phaenomena*.

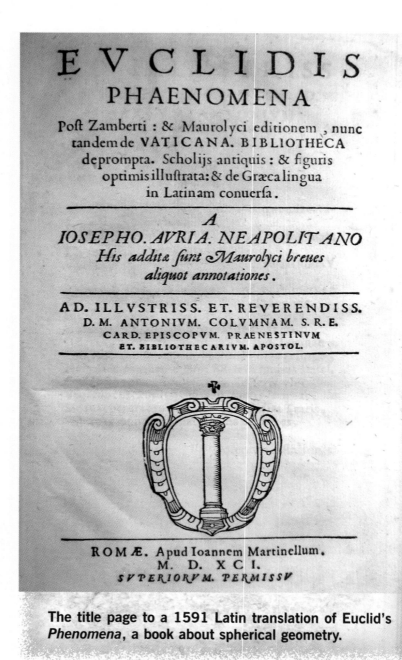

EVCLIDIS

PHAENOMENA

Poft Zamberti : & Maurolyci editionem , nunc
tandem de VATICANA. BIBLIOTHECA
deprompta. Scholijs antiquis : & figuris
optimis illuftrata: & de Græca lingua
in Latinam conuerfa.

A

IOSEPHO. AVRIA. NEAPOLITANO

*His addita funt Maurolyci breues
aliquot annotationes.*

AD. ILLVSTRISS. ET. REVERENDISS.
D. M. ANTONIVM. COLVMNAM. S. R. E.
CARD. EPISCOPVM. PRAENESTINVM
ET. BIBLIOTHECARIVM. APOSTOL.

ROMÆ. Apud Ioannem Martinellum.
M. D. X C I.
SVPERIORVM. PERMISSV

The title page to a 1591 Latin translation of Euclid's
Phenomena, a book about spherical geometry.

In ancient times, many astronomers believed that Earth was at the center of the universe. One ancient model of our universe had Earth surrounded by many concentric spheres, each incredibly large. The sun, moon, and other planets all existed on these universal spheres, moving along their surface, with each body having its own sphere. The stars in the background moved along the surface of the outermost sphere.

This model of the universe was known as the "doctrine of the spheres." Some ancient astronomers believed the motion of these heavenly bodies affected our lives here on Earth. Studying their exact positions and motion was regarded as an important task. Euclid's spherical geometry gave them the mathematics to calculate these data.[4]

It is almost strange that Euclid developed his spherical geometry. All of Euclid's geometric principles by definition apply to Euclidean space. However, the surface of a sphere is a non-Euclidean surface. The principles of the *Elements*

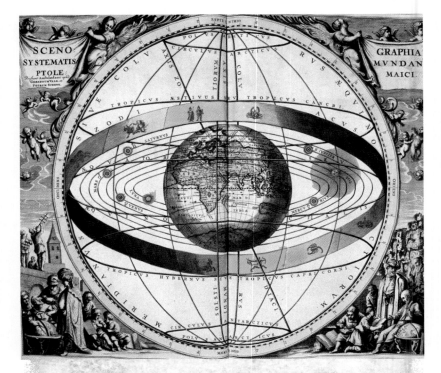

This illustration shows a geocentric model of the universe, similar to what many ancient astronomers believed. Earth is at the center, surrounded by the planets moving along their own paths and the stars (represented here by the signs of the Zodiac) traveling along the outermost orbit.

do not necessarily apply to shapes on the sphere's surface. Perhaps Euclid's spherical coordinates were his method to get around these exceptions to his geometry.

The Scientific Method

For more than a thousand years, Aristotle's work was the basis for science. Aristotle wrote many books about nature and the physical universe. The conclusions he reached about various topics came from logical thinking and observation of evidence. These books were used as science textbooks at most universities. Students were encouraged to read and memorize these works rather than experiment for themselves.

During the fifteenth century, Europe began a period known as the Renaissance, or "rebirth." This was a time of great learning and relearning, as Europe rediscovered classical texts from the Greeks and Romans. It was also a time of great scientific advancement and the beginnings of modern science itself.

Aristotle made claims based on pure logic and observation of the natural world. However, the new science of the Renaissance was based on evidence gathered from conducting experiments. This data had to be recorded carefully, and the new scientific concepts presented logically. Each conclusion required a strong foundation based on evidence and deduction.

As this new "scientific method" was gaining acceptance, the old ways of memorizing Aristotle's work and the work of other ancient Greek scientists were discarded. Gone were the ancient authorities, with their old conclusions based on logic. The new science demanded experiments, evidence, and proof. A new method of discovery was beginning.

Euclid was one of the ancient authors still studied even centuries later. His *Elements* was valued not just because it taught geometry but because it presented a very good model of a theorem. The model of a theorem was precisely what new scientists required. Propositions were presented and argued logically until a conclusion was proved based on evidence and logic.

Geometry in Engineering

Although geometry is largely a theoretical field, it has many applications for practical sciences. Any field of applied science that deals with physical relationships or structures has geometry as a basis. Structural engineering is the science of designing buildings and vehicles to support weight and different stresses. Geometry and structural engineering are closely tied together.

Structural engineering can be used to build a chair, an airplane, or a football stadium. Each of these items has an internal arrangement of supports and braces. These supports form different angles and shapes, each of which obeys geometric principles. Engineers can calculate the forces required to build these structures using basic geometry.

Geometry and engineering are also linked with architecture, or the science of constructing buildings and other structures. These fields of engineering work with many problems of angles, lines, and various shapes. The principles of geometry are as essential to these engineering fields as they are to shapes drawn on a piece of paper.

Because the *Elements* was studied so widely, Euclid has influenced almost every major scientist in history. This book was read and studied by Galileo Galilei. It was also read by Isaac Newton, who memorized each theorem as he read. It was studied by Nicolas Copernicus, Carl Friedrich Gauss, and Albert Einstein. The *Elements* influenced each of these scientists and taught them the principles of geometry and logical proof.

HISTORY VIEWS EUCLID

EUCLID'S *ELEMENTS* IS VALUED NOT ONLY because it is a textbook of geometry. It has been used by readers for centuries as a manual for logical thinking. The proofs and theorems that Euclid presented exercise the mind the same way that athletic games exercise the body. Scientists, mathematicians, and philosophers have used it to train themselves in logical thinking.

The American president Thomas Jefferson studied Euclid as a means of understanding the new science of his day. The methods Euclid used to prove mathematical truths are the same methods used to prove scientific truths. The later president Abraham Lincoln also studied the *Elements* to improve his logic as a lawyer and politician. Lincoln kept a copy of the *Elements* in his saddlebag as he traveled on horseback.[1]

Likewise, *Elements* has been studied by other mathematicians, philosophers, scientists, and everyday students for more than two thousand years. Some have studied it for the principles of geometry it contains. Others study it to train themselves in the principles of logic. Either way, the *Elements* has been the most important textbook in history.

Euclid's Other Books

Because Euclid's works were copied so often, his name as an author became famous. Other books were credited to him even though he did not write them. The *Elements* only contains thirteen chapters yet an additional Book XIV and Book XV have been found. These chapters also focus on similar geometric principles, but Euclid did not write them.

However, Euclid did write other books besides the *Elements*. One was his book *Optics*, and another was entitled *Catoptrica*, a second work on optics. This second book may be a later addition by another author named Hypsicles of Alexandria (about 190 to about 120 B.C.) and not Euclid's original work.[2] Several other books have been credited to Euclid by later translators. Some have now been proved to be the work of other authors.

Other books written by Euclid include *Phaenomena* on the subject of spherical geometry. He also wrote two other separate books on geometry entitled *Data* and *On Divisions*. These books were probably written to be used in addition to the *Elements*. They were possibly written at Alexandria to be used by students for the further study of geometry.

Euclid also wrote several other books that have since been lost. These books include *Conics, Pseudaria, Porisms,* and *Surfaces as Geometrical Loci*. Each of these books studied other topics of geometry or logic. We only know about these books because other ancient authors refer to them in their writings. However, copies of these books have never been found.

Authors of the Elements

Because the details of his life are so few, other theories have surfaced regarding the man known to us as Euclid. None of Euclid's original books of the *Elements* survives to this day. All we know of Euclid, and of the text of the *Elements,* comes from copies made centuries after he lived. No direct sources exist for Euclid or his writings.

Many critics view the *Elements* as a combination of other mathematicians' work. They see Euclid as borrowing theories and ideas already written by other authors. Some historians see Euclid as assembling and organizing previous mathematical ideas rather than writing his own. They believe Euclid may not have developed anything mathematically original.

Other historians believe the *Elements* could be a multiauthor work. Euclid taught many students and other mathematicians at Alexandria. The different books of the *Elements* could have been written by mathematicians under Euclid's direction. They would be collected later by their teacher, Euclid, who signed his name to the finished volume.[3]

A more curious theory is that the man known as Euclid did not exist at all. Sometimes authors write using another name because they want to remain anonymous. This happened in 1935 with the mathematician named Nicolas Bourbaki. "Bourbaki" was not a real person, just a name invented by a group of mathematicians who all used the same name for their writings.[4] Some scholars believe "Euclid" may have been just a name invented by a group of ancient mathematicians at Alexandria.

A few medieval translators named Euclid of Megara as the author of the *Elements*. They confused Euclid with another ancient Greek philosopher properly named Eucleides of Megara (about 400 B.C.). This author was a student of Socrates who lived approximately a century earlier than Euclid. Eucleides was more concerned with logic and philosophy than geometry.

Through the Centuries

Euclid's work continued to enjoy success far past his own life. Greek mathematicians continued to write commentaries about the *Elements* long after

Euclid died. Theon of Alexandria (circa A.D. 335–405) produced a new edition of the *Elements* in the fourth century A.D. A Roman senator named Boethius (circa A.D. 480–524) wrote his own interpretation of the *Elements* in Latin, although his version was rather poor.[5]

One of the reasons we have copies of Euclid's work today is that it was copied continuously. These copies spread as geometry textbooks, and they were translated into many languages. The first Arabic translation was by a scholar named al-Hajjaj ibn Yusuf ibn Matar about A.D. 800.[6] The *Elements* was used widely throughout the medieval Arab world.

The Arabs were especially interested in the content of the *Elements*. They had a strong interest in astronomy and astrology, the study of the positions of stars and planets. The geometric principles written by Euclid were very valuable to them. The Arab world was strong and successful while Europe was in the Dark Ages. This kept the knowledge of the *Elements* preserved so it could be reintroduced back to Europe.

The *Elements* was one of the first books printed after the invention of the printing press in 1454. The first printed version of the *Elements* was a Latin translation by Johannes Campanus of Venice in 1482. As a printed text, this book became even more widely read and studied. The first English version was published by Sir Henry Billingsley, later lord mayor of London, in 1570.[7]

The Only Geometry Book

Euclid's *Elements* has been used as a simple geometry text for thousands of years, virtually unchanged, and it influences geometry textbooks even today. It was so widely used and accepted for so long, many believed it was perfect. To challenge Euclid was like challenging the truth of mathematics itself.

We should not believe that Euclid's *Elements* is without mistakes. Over the centuries, many mathematicians have found small errors in his work. Sometimes Euclid repeats his ideas, and some pieces are unnecessary.[8] Some feel many of the postulates need more detailed proofs.

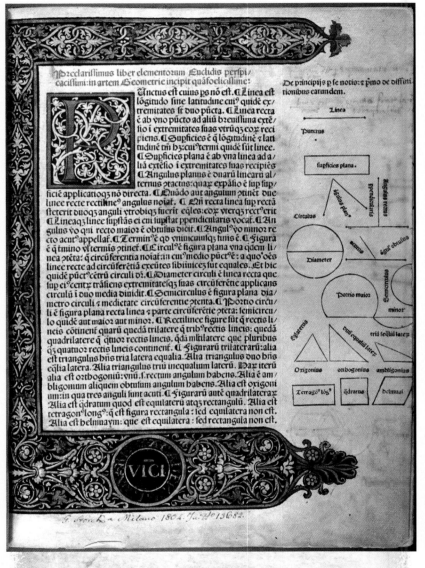

This is a page from the 1482 Latin translation of *Elements* by Johannes Campanus of Venice, the first printed version of the ancient text.

The title page to *The Elements of Geometry* by Sir Henry Billingsley, the first English translation, 1570.

However, Euclid's work is correct overall, and it is correct enough to be studied as truth.

The *Elements* has been very influential in many other areas of mathematics and science. It was studied by later important scientists, such as Nicolaus Copernicus, Galileo Galilei, and Isaac Newton. It has inspired the subjects of astronomy and many other areas of physics. The principles it includes have been used to build more complex mathematics, both Euclidean and non-Euclidean.

More than a thousand separate editions of Euclid's *Elements* are estimated to have been produced throughout history.[9] This fact makes the *Elements* second only to the Bible in the number of editions published. This book has been translated into every major language and adapted for readers of all ages. It remains today the best geometry book ever written.

ACTIVITIES

Constructing an Equilateral Triangle

An equilateral triangle is a triangle with all three sides having equal length. Because all three sides are equal, the three inside angles are also all equal. This activity is from Proposition 1 of Book I of the Elements.

Materials:

 ❖ a flat 12-inch ruler
 ❖ a drawing compass
 ❖ a pencil
 ❖ blank paper

Procedure:

1. Draw a short, straight line in the middle of the paper using the pencil and ruler. Any length will do, but make sure you leave enough room to work. Label the end points of this line A and B.

2. Open the compass to a width equal to the length of the line AB.

3. Place the point of the compass at the point A. Draw a circle with the compass using A as the center.

4. Using the same width, place the point of the compass at the point B. Draw a second identical circle with the compass using B as the center.

5. The two circles should intersect each other at two points. Label one of these points C.

6. Draw two straight lines connecting A to C and B to C. The figure ABC is an equilateral triangle.

7. Verify by measuring the sides of the triangle with the ruler to make sure they are all equal.

Constructing a Regular Hexagon

A hexagon is a polygon with six sides, from the Greek word *hex* meaning "six." If all six sides are equal and all six inside angles are equal, the hexagon is described as a regular hexagon. This activity is from Proposition 15 of Book IV of the *Elements*.

Materials
- ❖ a flat 12-inch ruler
- ❖ a drawing compass
- ❖ a pencil
- ❖ blank paper

Procedure

1. Draw a straight line across the middle of the paper using the pencil and ruler. Pick any point on this line and label it A.

2. Open the compass to a certain width. Any width will do, but make sure you leave enough room to work.

3. Place the point of the compass at point A. Draw a circle with the compass using A as the center. The circle should intersect the line at two points. Label these points B and C.

4. Using the same width, place the point of the compass at point B. Draw a second identical circle using B as the center. The two circles should intersect each other at two points. Label these two points D and E.

5. Using the ruler, draw a straight line through the points D and A. Extend this line until it reaches the other side of the circle. Label this new point of intersection as F.

6. Again, draw a second straight line through the points E and A. Extend this line until it reaches the other side of the

circle. Label this new point of intersection as G.

7. Connect the points B, D, G, C, F, and E with six straight lines using the ruler. The figure BDGCFE is a regular hexagon.

8. Verify by measuring the sides of the hexagon with the ruler to make sure they are all equal.

Constructing a Triangle From Three Lines

Three lines of any length can make a triangle, as long as two of the lines put together are longer than the third. Here any three lines that you draw can be used to construct a triangle. This activity is from Proposition 22 of Book I of the Elements.

Materials
- a flat 12-inch ruler
- a drawing compass
- a pencil
- blank paper

Procedure
1. Draw three straight lines in the corner of the paper with the pencil and ruler.

Make all three of different lengths, but do not make any much shorter than the others. Label these lines A, B, and C, with A the longest and C the shortest.

2. Draw a straight line across the middle of the paper using the pencil and ruler. Label one end point of this line D.

3. Open the compass to a width equal to the length of the line A, the longest.

4. Place the point of the compass at point D. Mark where the circle drawn by the compass intersects with the line. Label this point of intersection E.

5. Place the point of the compass at point E and draw a circle with E as the center.

6. Open the compass to a width equal to the length of the line B, the middle length.

7. Place the point of the compass at point E. Mark where the circle drawn by the compass intersects with the line. Label this point of intersection F.

8. Open the compass to a width equal to the length of the line C, the shortest.

9. Place the point of the compass at point F and draw a circle with F as the center.

10. The two circles should intersect each other at two points. Label one of these points G.

11. Draw two straight lines connecting E to G and F to G. The figure EFG is triangle with sides equal to the original lines A, B, and C.

12. Verify by measuring the sides of the triangle with the ruler to make sure they are the same lengths as your original lines.

CHRONOLOGY

c. 624 B.C.—Thales of Miletus is born.

c. 580 B.C.—Pythagoras of Samos is born.

548 B.C.—Thales of Miletus dies.

500 B.C.—Pythagoras of Samos dies.

c. 470 B.C.—Hippocrates of Chios is born.

c. 320 B.C.—Euclid is born.

Third century B.C.—The library at Alexandria is built.

48 B.C.—A large collection of scrolls from the library at Alexandria is burned by Julius Caesar.

Third century A.D.—Some historians theorize the library at Alexandria, or at least a part of it, is destroyed by the Roman emperor Aurelian.

c. 270 B.C.—Euclid dies.

290 A.D.—Pappus of Alexandria is born.

Fourth century A.D.—Theon of Alexandria produces a new version of the *Elements*.

A.D. 350—Pappus of Alexandria dies.

A.D. 391—Roman Emperor Theodosius I orders the daughter library at Alexandria destroyed.

A.D. **411**—Proclus is born.

A.D. **485**—Proclus dies.

A.D. **642**—Alexandria is sacked by Muslim invaders; some historians claim the library is ultimately destroyed at this time.

circa A.D. **800**—Al-Hajjaj produces the first Arabic translation of the *Elements*.

1482—Johannes Campanus produces the first printed version of the *Elements*.

1570—Sir Henry Billingsley publishes the first English version of the *Elements*.

1663—John Wallis tries to prove the Parallel Postulate.

1829—Nikolai Ivanovitch Lobachevsky publishes his ideas on non-Euclidean geometry.

1832—János Bolyai publishes his ideas on non-Euclidean geometry.

1855—Carl Friedrich Gauss introduces his non-Euclidean geometry.

1868—Georg Friedrich Bernhard Riemann's book *On the Foundation of Geometry* is published, further developing non-Euclidean mathematics.

1916—Albert Einstein publishes his general theory of relativity.

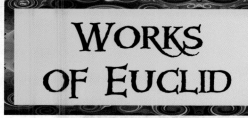
WORKS OF EUCLID

Stoicheia (Elements)

Consisting of thirteen separate books organizing the principles of geometry and logical mathematics.

Ta Dedomena (Data)[1]

This was a separate work of elementary geometry that included ninety-four propositions.[2]

Porismata (Porisms) (lost)[3]

This work of higher geometry dealt with a type of proposition somewhere between a theorem and a problem.

Peri Diaireseon (On Divisions)

This work on the division of figures is only known from an incomplete Arabic translation, for which only four of the included proofs survive.

Optika (Optics)

A study of rays of light from a geometry treatment.

Phainomena (Phaenomena)

An astronomy text dealing with spherical geometry based in part on a previous work by Autolycus of Pitane.[4]

IIII The Father of Geometry

Sectio Canonis (Elements of Music)

This work on music may be the rewrite of an original Euclid text by a later, unknown writer. Very little of the original text by Euclid is believed to remain.[5]

Surfaces as Geometrical Loci (lost)

A discussion of the relationships of points on solid surfaces.

Elements of Conic Sections (Conics) (lost)

This lost book provided the basis for a later book of the same title by Apollonius of Perga.

Pseudaria or Pseudographemata (Fallacies) (lost)

This book exposed fallacies in geometrical reasoning.

CHAPTER NOTES

Chapter 1. The Life of Euclid

1. Sir Thomas Heath, *A History of Greek Mathematics, Volume I: From Thales to Euclid* (New York: Dover, 1981), p. 358.

2. Vivian Shaw Groza, *A Survey of Mathematics: Elementary Concepts and Their Historical Development* (New York: Holt, Rinehart & Winston, 1968), p. 99.

3. John McLeish, *Number: From Ancient Civilisations to the Computer* (London: HarperCollins, 1991), p. 85.

4. Frank N. Magill, ed., *The Great Scientists, Vol. 4: Dedekind–Fracastoro* (Danbury, Conn.: Grolier Educational, 1989), p. 142.

5. James R. Newman, *The World of Mathematics* (New York: Simon and Schuster, 1956), vol. 1, p. 100.

6. Heath, p. 354.

7. Groza, pp. 99–100.

Chapter 2. Geometry Before Euclid

1. Leonard Mloinow, *Euclid's Window: The Story of Geometry From Parallel Lines to Hyperspace* (New York: Free Press, 2001), pp. 6, 14.

2. Arnold Reymond, *History of the Sciences in Greco-Roman Antiquity*, trans. Ruth Gheury de Bray (New York: Bibio and Tannen, 1963), p. 57.

3. Carl B. Boyer, *A History of Mathematics* (New York: John Wiley and Sons, 1968), p. 50.

4. Ibid., p. 54.

5. Ibid., p. 57.

6. Reymond, p. 118.

7. Boyer, p. 115.

Chapter 3. Plane Geometry

1. Carl B. Boyer, *A History of Mathematics* (New York: John Wiley and Sons, 1968), p. 124.
2. Petr Beckman, *A History of Pi* (New York: St. Martin's Press, 1971), p. 50.
3. Leonard Mlodinow, *Euclid's Window: The Story of Geometry From Parallel Lines to Hyperspace* (New York: Free Press, 2001), p. 35.
4. Sir Thomas Heath, *A History of Greek Mathematics, Volume I: From Thales to Euclid* (New York: Dover, 1981), p. 379.
5. Boyer, pp. 252–253.
6. Ibid., p. 124.

Chapter 4. The Theory of Numbers

1. Thomas L. Heath, *A Manual of Greek Mathematics* (New York: Dover, 1963), p. 11.
2. Arnold Reymond, *History of the Sciences in Greco-Roman Antiquity,* trans. Ruth Gheury de Bray (New York: Bibio and Tannen, 1963), p. 60.
3. Reymond, pp. 125–126.
4. Carl B. Boyer, *A History of Mathematics* (New York: John Wiley and Sons, 1968), p. 128.
5. Reymond, p. 126.
6. Heath, p. 402.
7. Boyer, p. 129.

Chapter 5. Solid Geometry

1. Carl B. Boyer, *A History of Mathematics* (New York: John Wiley and Sons, 1968), p. 111.
2. David C. Lindberg, *The Beginnings of Western Science: The European Scientific Tradition in Philosophical, Religious, and Institutional Context, 600 B.C. to A.D. 1450* (Chicago: University of Chicago Press, 1992), p. 88.
3. Boyer, p. 130.

4. Ibid., p. 93.

5. Ibid., p. 94.

6. Lindberg, p. 88.

7. Leonard Mlodinow, *Euclid's Window: The Story of Geometry From Parallel Lines to Hyperspace* (New York: Free Press, 2001), p. 34.

Chapter 6. Euclid's Parallel Postulate

1. Leonard Mlodinow, *Euclid's Window: The Story of Geometry From Parallel Lines to Hyperspace* (New York: Free Press, 2001), pp. 118–119.

2. Ibid., p. 37.

3. Carl B. Boyer, *A History of Mathematics* (New York: John Wiley and Sons, 1968), p. 116.

4. Mlodinow, p. 104.

5. Vivian Shaw Groza, *A Survey of Mathematics: Elementary Concepts and Their Historical Development* (New York: Holt, Rinehart and Winston, 1968), pp. 287–288.

6. Mlodinow, p. 203.

Chapter 7. Euclid and the Sciences

1. James R. Newman, *The World of Mathematics* (New York: Simon and Schuster, 1956), vol. 1, p. 193.

2. Frank N. Magill, ed., *The Great Scientists, Vol. 4: Dedekind–Fracastoro* (Danbury, Conn.: Grolier Educational, 1989), p. 144.

3. David C. Lindberg, *The Beginnings of Western Science: The European Scientific Tradition in Philosophical, Religious, and Institutional Context, 600 B.C. to A.D. 1450* (Chicago: University of Chicago Press, 1992), pp. 105–106.

4. Giorgio Abetti, *The History of Astronomy*, trans. Betty Burr Abeitti (New York: Henry Schuman, 1952), p. 38.

Chapter 8. History Views Euclid

1. Drew R. McCoy, "An 'Old-Fashioned' Nationalism: Lincoln, Jefferson, and the Classical Tradition," *Journal of the Abraham Lincoln Association*, Winter 2002.

2. Frank N. Magill, ed., *The Great Scientists, Vol. 4: Dedekind–Fracastoro* (Danbury, Conn.: Grolier Educational, 1989), p. 144.

3. Jean Itard, *Les Livres Arithmétique d'Euclide* Revue d'Histoire des Sciences et de Leurs Applications, volume 17, 1964, pp. 170–171.

4. Carl B. Boyer, *A History of Mathematics* (New York: John Wiley and Sons, 1968), p. 674.

5. Leonard Mlodinow, *Euclid's Window: The Story of Geometry From Parallel Lines to Hyperspace* (New York: Free Press, 2001), pp. 45–46.

6. Magill, p. 145.

7. Marie Boas, *The Scientific Renaissance: 1450–1630* (New York: Harper and Row, 1962), p. 197.

8. John McLeish, *Number: From Ancient Civilisations to the Computer* (London: HarperCollins, 1991), p. 86.

9. Lucas N. H. Bunt, Phillip S. Jones, and Jack D. Bedient, *The Historical Roots of Elementary Mathematics* (Mineola, N.Y.: Dover, 1988), p. 142.

Works of Euclid

1. Arnold Reymond, *History of the Sciences in Greco-Roman Antiquity,* trans. Ruth Gheury de Bray (New York: Bibio and Tannen, 1963), pp. 69–70.

2. Frank N. Magill, ed., *The Great Scientists, Vol. 4: Dedekind–Fracastoro* (Danbury, Conn.: Grolier Educational, 1989), p. 144.

3. Thomas L. Heath, *A Manual of Greek Mathematics* (New York: Dover, 1963), pp. 255–269.

4. Magill, p. 144.

5. Ibid.

GLOSSARY

angle—A figure formed by two lines crossing at a common point.

axiom—A statement commonly believed to be true without proof.

circumscribe—To draw something on the outside of a closed figure.

city-state—An independent, self-governing city of ancient Greece.

conics—Shapes produced when a two-dimensional plane intersects a cone.

deduction—A logical reasoning using basic concepts to prove more complex ideas in a step-by-step manner.

dimension—An independent direction in space.

equilateral—Having all sides equal.

geometry—The study of shapes, lines, and angles and their relationships.

greatest common divisor (GCD)—The largest factor that is common between two whole numbers.

inscribe—To draw something on the inside of a closed figure.

intersection—The point at which two lines or curves cross or touch.

irrational number—A number that cannot be written as a ratio of two whole numbers.

least common multiple (LCM)—The smallest whole number of which both of two numbers are a divisor.

method of exhaustion—A technique of calculating the area of a circle by an inscribed polygon with an increasing number of sides.

museum—An institution dedicated to collecting, preserving and studying objects of art, science, and history.

parallel—Spaced perfectly apart at all points, never intersecting.

perfect numbers—Whole numbers whose value is equal to the sum of their divisors.

perspective—The appearance of objects as different depending on their distance from the viewer.

plane—A two-dimensional surface that is perfectly flat and infinite in all directions.

plane geometry—The study of shapes and principles within a two-dimensional plane.

polygon—A closed figure with many straight sides.

postulate—Another name for an axiom.

prime number—A number that only has divisors of itself and 1.

ratio—The measure of the relative size of two magnitudes.

solid geometry—The study of three-dimensional solid objects and their principles.

spherical geometry—The study of the two-dimensional surface of a sphere.

tangent—A straight line that touches a circle at just one point.

theorem—A statement logically proven to be true in a step-by-step proof.

FURTHER READING

Books

Hayhurst, Chris. *Euclid: The Great Geometer*. New York: Rosen, 2006.

Heath, T. L. *Euclid's Elements*. Santa Fe, N. Mex.: Green Lion Press, 2002.

Leech, Bonnie Coulter. *Geometry's Great Thinkers: The History of Geometry*. New York: Rosen Publishing Group's PowerKids Press, 2006.

Staeger, Rob. *Ancient Mathematicians*. Greensboro, N.C.: Morgan Reynolds Pub., 2008.

Venkatraman, Padma. *Women Mathematicians*. Greensboro, N.C. : Morgan Reynolds Pub., 2009.

INTERNET ADDRESSES

Biography of Euclid
http://www.mathopenref.com/euclid.html

**Euclid's Elements—A Quick Trip through
the Elements**
http://aleph0.clarku.edu/~djoyce/java/elements/trip.
html

**neoK—12: Educational Videos and Lessons for
K-12 School Kids—Plane Geometry**
http://www.neok12.com/Geometry.htm

INDEX